NOW YOU CAN READ...
STORIES FROM THE BIBLE

THOMAS NELSON PUBLISHERS · NASHVILLE · CAMDEN · NEW YORK

Publishers since 1798

CONTENTS

Noah and the Ark

Once, long long ago, an old man,
with a long beard and snowy-white
hair, was cutting tree trunks into
planks. Many people stood round him
watching to see what he was making.
The man's name was Noah. Noah was
a good man who loved God.

Noah's wife and his three sons watched him work. At last, they saw what he was making. It was a very large, strong ship.

"How can it float?" said Noah's wife. "There is no water nearby." Noah said, "This is a new kind of ship called an ark. It will have a door in the side and a roof. It will have a window and three decks."

"What is it for, husband? Why are you making the ark?" said Noah's wife.

"God has told me to make the ark," said Noah. "He will send rain which will cover the land. Every living thing will die because His people have been wicked. We must go inside the ark with our sons and their wives. We must take with us two of every kind of animal. The ark will float on the water and all inside it will be safe."

"We will need food for everyone
and food for the animals," said
Noah's wife. So, Noah and his wife
and three sons began to make plans
for their stay in the ark.

Sacks of grain and bags of salt
were put on the deck of the ark.
Barrels of fresh water for drinking
were filled. Hay and straw for the
animals were laid inside the ark.

They found the animals and took them onto the ark. There was every kind of animal there, elephants, lions and camels.

There were dogs, cats, birds,
snakes and even mice and worms.

Noah told everyone to hurry, for
he sensed that the rain was coming
soon. He pushed two donkeys from
behind. "Come along, you slow
donkeys, get on board if you do
not want to get your feet wet!"

When everyone and everything was inside, the Lord closed the door. Soon, great black clouds filled the sky and rain began to fall.

Day after day it rained, until all the land was covered with water. The rain fell for forty days and forty nights. The ark was lifted. It floated high in the water.

The water covered the land for many, many days. Inside the ark, everyone was becoming tired, for it was noisy and there was little food left.

A dog growled, as if to say, "My straw is not soft. I cannot sleep."

On the other side of the ark, the giraffes were very unhappy. The roof was so low that they had to bend their heads. They had very stiff necks.

At last, the rain stopped, and the
waters went down. The ark came to
rest upon a mountain. Noah looked
out to see how he could tell
when it would be safe to leave
the ark.

He went to where the birds rested and spoke to the big, black raven. "Go out, raven and fly over the land. If you can find a tree in which to rest, then stay there. If you cannot find a tree, then fly back to the ark." The raven was away all day. It did not come back. "I will wait a little longer," said Noah.

A week later, Noah
sent out a dove.

The little dove
came back to the
ark, for she knew
there was food
there.
"I will wait a
little longer,"
said Noah. "I
think things will
be better soon."

He waited seven days and let the
dove out again.
When night came, Noah saw the dove
coming back. It held in its beak
a green olive leaf.

"The leaves have grown again on
the trees," cried Noah. "Now we
can leave the ark."

The door was opened. Noah and his
family came out of the ark.

The animals and
birds were glad
to be free again
on dry land.
God had spared
Noah, and all his
family from the
flood. They gave
thanks to God.

"Look! Look up there in the sky," cried Noah's wife. Right across the sky was a lovely rainbow. This was God's promise that He would never again flood the world.
Sometimes, when it has been raining, if you look up into the sky, you too, can see a rainbow.

27

All these appear in the pages of the story. Can you find them?

Noah

Noah's wife

ark

two donkeys

rainbow

dove

mountain

rain

Now tell the story in your own words.

Moses in the Bulrushes

Long ago, in a country called Egypt, there lived a girl named Miriam. She was twelve years old. Her hair was long and dark, and her face was gentle. She had a brother called Aaron. He was a good boy and helped his father with the work. Their mother had another child, a little boy. He was a happy baby. He laughed and smiled at them from his cradle.

They all lived in a small, dark
house, near a great river called
the Nile. It was warm during the
day but cold at night, in that
little house.

Not far away stood a great white
palace. It was where the king
lived. He was the ruler of Egypt
and he was a proud and cruel man.
He wanted to be king of Egypt for
as long as he lived. He did not
want anyone else to take his place.

Miriam's people had come from a land called Israel, and they were God's chosen people, but the king did not like them. He made them work very hard, and he said that all their baby boys had to be killed.

Outside the big white palace marched the soldiers who guarded the king. They were hard and cruel like the king.

When they heard what the king wanted, they said they would help him. They would go to the houses and take away every baby boy. They would throw them into the river.

Miriam said, "What shall we do, mother? I do not want the soldiers to find my little brother and take him away."

"Do not be afraid, Miriam," said her mother. "I have a plan, wait and see."

When the baby was three months old, he was a strong child and his crying was very loud. His mother was worried that one of the king's cruel soldiers would hear him.

She picked some bulrushes from behind the house.

She made a basket, shaped like a cradle. On the outside, she spread black tar, so that the water could not get in. Inside, she put a lovely soft cloth.

Then, very gently, she put the baby into the basket and called to Miriam. "Come with me and be very quiet. I want you to help me and do what I say."

They crept down to the side of
the river and looked for a good
place to put the basket. It could
not go where the water ran or it
would float away.

They hid the basket in a clump of
bulrushes and Miriam sat down behind
it.

"You must stay here, Miriam," said her mother. "Watch the basket. This is just the place where the king's daughter comes to swim. She will find your little brother here. She will take him to the palace. If she does, then he will be safe."

Miriam sat very still behind the
bulrushes. She was afraid.
Before long, she
heard voices and
girls laughing.
The princess was
walking along the
path. A slave
held a sun-shade
over her.

Miriam held her breath. Her little brother had begun to cry, for he was hungry by that time.

"What's that?" called the princess. "A basket is hidden there. Go and bring it to me."

One of the servant girls paddled out into the water.

She lifted up the basket and took it back to the princess. She lifted the lid. There was the poor baby, crying and kicking his legs.

The princess didn't know much about babies, but she picked him up and cuddled him. Soon he was quiet.

"What a lovely child!" she cried.
"I would like to keep him."

Miriam stood up
and walked
forward.
"Do you need a
nurse for your
baby? I know
someone who
would be pleased
to help you," she
said.
"Yes," said the
princess. "I do
need a nurse.
Will you bring
her to me?"

Miriam ran home and told her mother what had happened. They hurried back to where the princess was waiting.

"You may take him away and look after him," said the princess to Miriam's mother. "I shall see that you are paid. When he is older you must bring him back to me."

So Miriam, the
baby and their
mother went back
to the dark,
little house.
They lived
there safely.
When the baby
was older, his
mother took
him to the
palace. The
princess loved
the little boy
and she called
him Moses.

All these appear in the pages of
the story. Can you find them?

mother

Miriam

king

baby

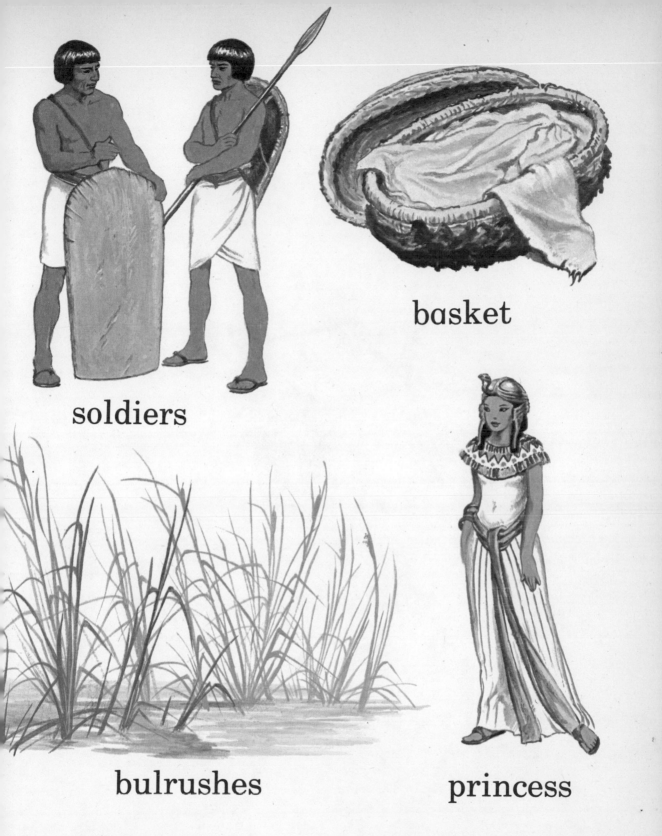

soldiers

basket

bulrushes

princess

Now tell the story in your own words.

Moses the Leader

A boy called Moses lived in a great palace. It was the home of the king of Egypt. The king's daughter had looked after Moses since he was a baby. She had found Moses lying in a cradle. It was hidden in the bulrushes near the river. His mother had hidden him there. She was afraid of the cruel king. The king's name was Pharaoh.

As she sat by a pool, the princess talked to Moses about his people. Many years ago, she said, Moses' people had to come to Egypt to look for food. The king had made them slaves. He made them work very hard.

When Moses became older, he went out to watch the slaves. They made bricks with clay and straw and water. The wet bricks dried in the hot sun. Pharaoh made the slaves build great cities. If they stopped to rest, his cruel soldiers hit them with whips. Moses was sad because his people were not free. One day he killed a soldier who was hitting one of his people. Pharaoh was very angry.

Moses left the palace. He went across the desert into another land. Many years passed. Moses became a shepherd. One day, as he was looking after his sheep on the hillside, God sent him a sign. Moses saw a bush in front of him. It burst into flames but the flames did not burn the bush.

A voice called to Moses. It came from the middle of the bush.

"Moses, take off your shoes and come near. This is holy ground." It was the voice of God.

Moses knelt before the burning bush. God told him to lead his people out of Egypt to a new land. They would be free. He told Moses to go back to Egypt and ask Pharaoh to let the people go.

Moses went back to Egypt. He found his brother Aaron. They called the slaves together to tell them what God had said.

The people bowed their heads and gave thanks to God.

Moses and Aaron went to the palace.
They came before the king to tell
him of God's words.

Pharaoh became
very angry.
"Why should I
listen to your
God? I need
slaves to work
for me. I will
never let them
go!"

Pharaoh had his soldiers beat the slaves so they would work harder. God punished Pharaoh. He made Pharaoh's people and their animals sick. The king's people became afraid. They begged Pharaoh to let the slaves go.

"Go," Pharaoh said to Moses. "Take your children and your animals. Go from this land."

Moses helped his people make ready to leave. They tied things in bundles. Cattle and sheep were herded together. Their cooking pots and water jars were slung across oxen. They then made their way on foot, out of the land of Egypt. They had been slaves for more than four hundred years.

Moses led his people across the desert. There was little water or food. The children cried. They were hot and tired. The people were afraid.

"Do not be afraid," said Moses. "God will show us the way."

God did not forget them. By day, He sent a pillar of cloud in front of them. It showed them the way to go.

At night, a pillar of fire glowed in the dark, so that they could see.

In Egypt, people
were angry.
Without the slaves,
there was no one
to do the work.
Pharaoh sent all
his soldiers to
bring back
the slaves.

Moses and his people came to the Red Sea. They could not cross the sea. They said to Moses, "Why have you led us here to die?"

"God will help us," said Moses. God put a pillar of cloud between them and Pharaoh's army. The soldiers could not see them.

Then God said to Moses, "Lift your staff over the sea. The sea will part and leave a path in the middle. Your people can cross to the other side."

Moses did as he was told. There came a mighty wind. The sea rolled back.

Moses and his people crossed to
the other side. They saw Pharaoh's
men follow. What could they do?
They were lost.

God told Moses to stretch his hand over the sea. When he did so, the waves crashed like thunder. The waters of the sea came together. The sea covered the wicked soldiers. Not one was left.

Moses and his people fell onto
their knees to thank God. God had
saved them. They were free. At
last they were going to the land
God had given them.

All these appear in the pages of
the story. Can you find them?

Princess

Moses

Pharaoh

slaves

bush

soldiers

pillar of cloud   waves

Now tell the story in your own words.

Samuel

One day, in a place called Shiloh,
the people took their children to
pray in God's house. It was called
the Temple.

The Temple was a holy place. Inside was an altar of wood and a shining lamp. Behind the altar, a tent hid the Ark of God. Inside the Ark, lay the holy laws God had given to the people.

When the people came out of the Temple, they had a great feast.

The children sang and had a happy time.

One woman, whose name was Hannah, sat alone. She had no children. She wished that she could have just one child. Year after year she waited. No child was born. Hannah was very sad.

She left the feast and walked back to the Temple. At the door, sat the old priest Eli. Hannah walked past him and knelt down.

She prayed to God. She asked Him to send her a baby. "If I have a son," she said, "I will give him back to You. He will do Your work."

Eli went up to her and said,
"What is the matter?"
She told him and he said,
"Go in peace. May God give you
what you want."
Hannah felt happy as she went back
to the feast.
Very soon, God gave Hannah a little
son. She called him Samuel.

She did not forget her promise to
God. While Samuel was still very
young, she made him a little coat.
She took him with her to the
Temple.
She went to Eli
and said,
"I am the woman
who asked God for
a son. God has
heard my prayer.
This is the boy
He sent me. Now
I am giving him
back to God as
I promised."

Samuel was a good boy. Eli looked after him as if he were his own. Every year, his mother went to see him. She took him a new coat.

Samuel helped Eli each day in the Temple.

Eli had two sons.
They did not help
him. They made
fun of holy things
and spent their
time in Shiloh.
Eli knew that his
sons did wicked
things, but he
said nothing.

Eli was very old
and nearly blind.
Samuel led Eli
everywhere.

Samuel slept in a corner of the Temple, near the lamp of gold. He had to see that the lamp was always kept burning. Samuel kept the oil ready.

One night, he woke up. He heard
a voice calling "Samuel, Samuel."
He thought it was
Eli calling him.
He ran through the
Temple to where
Eli lay.
"I did not call
you," Eli said.
"Go back to sleep."

85

Again the voice called and once again, Samuel ran to Eli.
"I did not call you," said Eli.

When the voice called a third time, Eli knew that it was God who spoke to the boy. He said, "If you hear the voice again, you must say, 'Speak, Lord, I can hear You'."

Samuel did as Eli told him. He was not afraid. He waited. All was still in the Temple. The lamp glowed softly. God spoke to Samuel and said, "The sons of Eli are very wicked. Eli knows this. I shall punish Eli and his sons. You must tell Eli what I have said."

Samuel was sad. He loved Eli. He did not want to tell him what God had said. So Samuel lay down until morning.

Then, as Eli sat under a great
tree outside the Temple, Samuel told
him God's words. Eli put his hands
over his face.
"God will do what is right," he
said at last.

At night in the Temple, God spoke many times to Samuel. People came from far away to hear Samuel. He told the people what God wanted them to do.

The years went by and war broke out. The people sent a message to the Temple. They wanted the Ark. They thought that God would help them if they carried it. Eli's wicked sons took the Ark from the Temple.

The Ark was carried into battle.

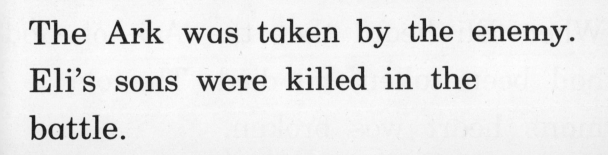

The Ark was taken by the enemy.
Eli's sons were killed in the
battle.

A man who had been in the fighting
came to tell Eli about the battle.
He found Eli sitting beside the road.

When Eli heard that the Ark of God
had been taken, he died. The old
man's heart was broken.

Samuel prayed to God to help the people. He told them to serve God. The people listened to Samuel for he spoke the word of God.

All these appear in the pages of the story. Can you find them?

Temple

Ark

lamp

children

Hannah

Eli

sons

Samuel

Now tell the story in your own words.

David and Goliath

David was a shepherd boy. He looked after his father's sheep. He had to see that no one came to steal the sheep. If a wild animal came close, he had to chase it away. David had seven brothers. He was the youngest in the family.

One day, as he was
tending the sheep in
the field, he saw
someone coming. He
jumped up and ran
to meet him. It
was one of his
father's servants.

The servant said, "Leave the sheep, David. Come back to your father's house. Someone wants to see you. I will look after the sheep while you are gone."

David ran quickly to the house.

His face was red as he ran inside.

His father was standing next to
another man, and said to David,
"This man is called Samuel. He
wants to meet you. He has a
special job for you to do."

101

Samuel knew that when David grew up, he would be the king of the country. He was still a boy, but God had told Samuel that David was His choice for the next king. Samuel put oil on David's head to show he was God's choice.

Samuel talked to David and then he went away.

At that time, the king of the country was a man called Saul. He was not a very good king. Sometimes he felt unhappy and would not speak to anyone. "Perhaps if someone played some cheerful music for King Saul, it would make him feel happy," said one of the servants.

David could play lovely music on the
harp. He was asked to go to the
palace and play for King Saul. He
played some happy music and sang
songs and soon the King was more
cheerful.

"I want you to stay here at the palace," said King Saul. "Send a message to your father to tell him where you are."

David liked being at the palace. He talked to the King about his home and the lambs in the fields. Soon after David had gone to the palace, war broke out. King Saul had to get his army ready.

Three of David's brothers were in the army, so he had to go back to his father.

One day, David took some new bread to his brothers. He liked to go and see the soldiers.

David was talking to
his brothers when
a great shout was
heard. A huge man,
a giant, was walk-
ing towards
them.

"Who will fight
with me?" he roared.
"If he wins, then
you have won this
battle, but if I
win, then you will
all be in our
power."

"Who is going to fight him?" asked
David.

"No one dares to fight Goliath,"
said one of the soldiers. "No one
could stand up to a man like that."
David knew at once what he should
do. He went to King Saul.

"I will fight Goliath," he said.

"You!" cried King Saul. "You are only a youth. Goliath is a real fighter. You cannot fight him."

"I may be small," said David, "but with God's help I have killed bears and lions when they came to steal my father's sheep. Please, let me try."

King Saul took off the suit of
armour which he was wearing and pu
it on David. It was much too big.
He tripped over it.

"I cannot wear this," said David.
"It is too heavy and too big.
Please take it off." The armour
was taken off and David felt much
better.

He took his sling and went to a little stream nearby. He chose five smooth stones and put them in a bag. Then he walked towards the giant.

Goliath could not
believe his eyes.
A little boy was
coming to fight
him! He put down
his great head and
charged. David
took one of the
stones out of his
bag and put it in
his sling.

He spun the sling
around his head,
faster and faster
and let it go.

The stone flew through the air and
hit Goliath right in the middle of
his forehead. He crashed to the
ground like a fallen tree.

David ran up to him and took the sword from Goliath's side. With one blow he cut off Goliath's head. All the soldiers cheered and shouted. The enemy turned and ran away.

King Saul spoke to David. "You shall stay with us now. You will not return to your father's house. My son, Jonathan, will be a good friend to you."

Jonathan was very kind to David and they became like brothers.

All these appear in the pages of the story. Can you find them?

David

sheep

King Saul

Samuel

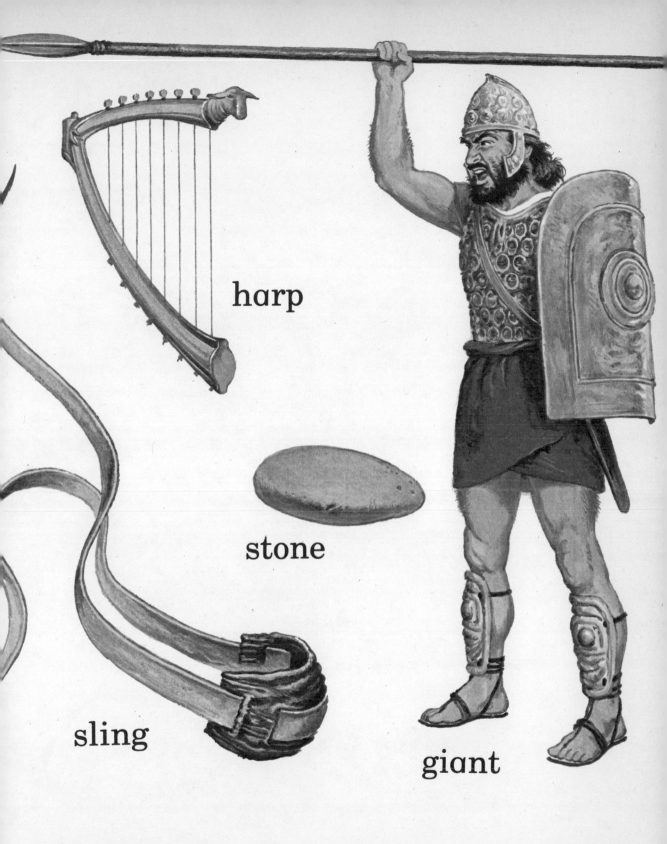

harp

stone

sling

giant

Now tell the story in your own words.

David and Jonathan

David was a young shepherd boy.
His father had eight sons and he
was the youngest. The older boys
became soldiers in the king's army.
David was left at home to look
after the sheep.

One day, a stranger named Samuel came to David's home. He told David that God had chosen David to be a king when he was older. David was surprised, but he did not say anything.

Some time later, David was taken to
see the king of the country who
was King Saul. David was very good
at playing the harp. King Saul
liked to listen to him play. He
asked David to stay at the palace
with him.

David was a gentle boy and a brave one too. Once, a great giant named Goliath, came with his army against King Saul. No one dared to face the giant, but with God's help, David stood up to him. He killed Goliath with a stone thrown from his sling. King Saul made David a leader in his army.

When the army came home after the battle, people came out of their houses. They danced and sang in the streets. Everyone was happy. The people loved David. Everyone said how brave he had been. King Saul was very angry. He was afraid the people would make David king in his place.

From that time, whenever King Saul saw David, he became angry.

One day, the King threw a spear at David to pin him to the wall. David ran from the room. David became very unhappy living at the palace. He became afraid of King Saul.

Jonathan, the King's son, was kind. He was a good friend to David. They made a promise to each other that, whatever happened, they would always be friends.

David wanted to leave the palace. He was afraid King Saul would kill him. But Jonathan did not want him to go. "My father will not hurt you," he said. "He always tells me what he wants to do."

But David was still afraid. He knew that he was in real danger.

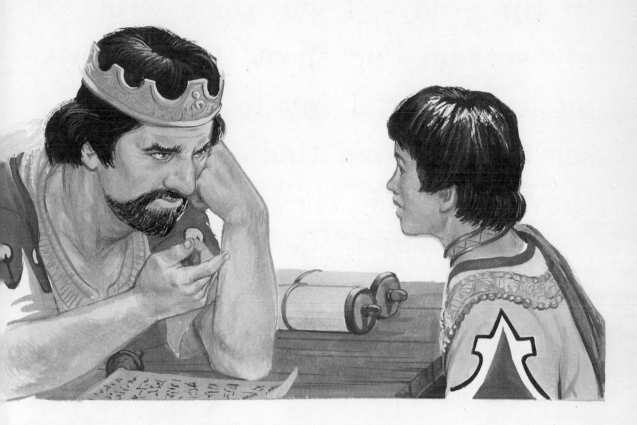

King Saul came to hate David. He told Jonathan to kill him. But Jonathan loved David and so he made a plan.

"In a field not far from here, there is a great stone," said Jonathan. "Go and hide behind it. In three days, I will come with my servant and shoot three arrows by its side. If I say to my servant, 'Go and find the arrows, they are beside the great stone,' then you will know that all is well. But, if I say, 'Find the arrows, they are ahead of you,' then you will know that there is great danger. You must go away."

So David hid behind the great
stone. Jonathan went to King Saul.
He begged him not to kill David.
King Saul did not listen. He
became very angry. He threw his
sword at Jonathan, but it missed
him.

Jonathan ran from the palace, calling his servant. He went to the field near the great stone. Soon his arrows flew through the air.

"Find the arrows,"
called Jonathan.
"They are ahead
of you!"

David heard and he was very sad.
The servant found the arrows.
Jonathan sent him home.

Then David came out of his hiding place. He put his arms round Jonathan.

"My father is so angry. I am sure he plans to kill you. You must go away," said Jonathan. "Hide far away from here. You must remember our promise. We shall always be friends."

David ran away. He found a cave
near the desert, where he lived
for a long time.

Other men who were afraid of King Saul joined David. He became their leader.

One day, someone
asked to see
David.

It was Jonathan. A long time had
passed. They were happy to meet
again. They threw their arms round
each other.

"You need not be afraid," said Jonathan. "My father will never find you. One day, you will be king and I shall serve you. Until then, we must part."

Jonathan went back to join his father's army.

Some years later, David heard that there had been a great battle. One day, a soldier from King Saul's camp came to David. His clothes were torn. David could see that he had been in the fighting. He told David that King Saul and Jonathan were dead. He brought the King's crown with him. He gave it to David.

David wept. He was very, very sad. God had made him a king, but David had lost his best and dearest friend.

All these appear in the pages of the story. Can you find them?

Jonathan

Goliath

David

King Saul

arrows

the great stone

crown

cave

Now tell the story in your own words.

The Birth of Jesus

Long ago, in a small town called Nazareth, there lived a girl named Mary. At that time, many men had forgotten about God. He decided to send His own Son to be born and grow up among the people. God's Son would teach them about His heavenly Father.

God knew that Mary loved Him, so
He chose her to be the mother of
His Son. He sent an angel called
Gabriel to tell Mary about the baby.
Mary was alone in
her house when she
saw the angel
standing beside her.
She was afraid and
hid her eyes.

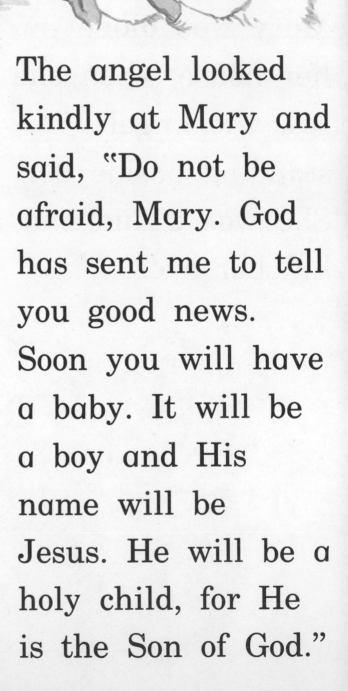

The angel looked kindly at Mary and said, "Do not be afraid, Mary. God has sent me to tell you good news. Soon you will have a baby. It will be a boy and His name will be Jesus. He will be a holy child, for He is the Son of God."

In the same town, a carpenter called Joseph lived. Joseph took Mary to be his wife. He wanted to take care of Mary and the baby, because he loved her.

The king of the land wanted all the people to be counted, so Mary and Joseph had to go back to the place where they were born.

It was a long way to go, so they had a little donkey for Mary to ride while Joseph walked by her side. At last, they came to an inn.

They were very tired and needed a rest. Joseph knocked at the door. The door opened and the inn-keeper said, "What do you want?"

"Have you a bed for the night, please?" asked Joseph. "My wife is very tired, for we have come a long way."

"I am very sorry," said the inn-keeper, shaking his head. "There is no room for you here. If you would like to stay in the stable with the animals, you are welcome to rest there. It is warm and dry." "Thank you," said Joseph. "That will do very well."

They followed the inn-keeper to the
stable, and there in the night, the
baby Jesus was born.

There was nothing for the baby to wear. Mary wrapped Him in strips of cloth. There was nowhere for the baby to sleep. Joseph made Him a little bed in the place where food for the cows and donkeys was kept. It was called a manger. He put warm, dry straw in it and Mary laid the baby there to sleep.

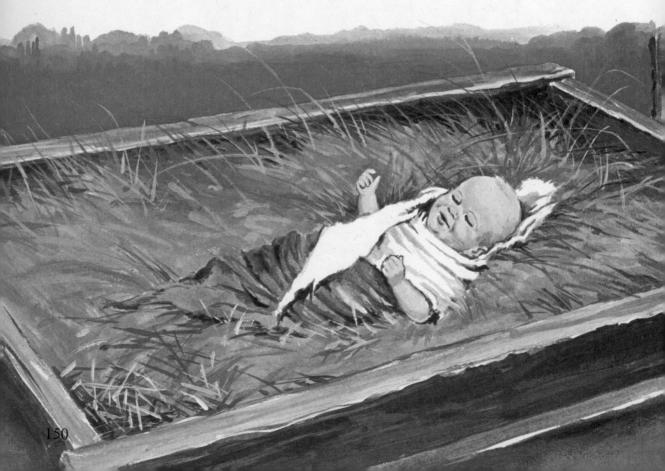

Outside, the night was dark and cold. In the fields close to the town, some shepherds were looking after their sheep. They sat close to the fire, warming their hands and talking to each other.

Suddenly, a great light shone in the sky and an angel stood in front of them.

They were all afraid but the angel said,

"Do not be afraid, for I have come to tell you good news. Tonight, the Lord Jesus has been born. Go to Him. You will find Him in the town, wrapped in pieces of cloth and lying in a manger."

Then the sky was filled with angels who sang,

"Glory to God in heaven
Peace on earth
And joy to all men"

At once the shepherds set off for the town. They went to the place where the angel had told them they would find the baby Jesus. They took their sheep with them in case a wolf should attack them.

The shepherds knocked
at the stable door
and Joseph let them
in.

They knelt down
beside the baby
because they knew
He was very special.

Mary was glad to have the shepherds come to see her baby, the newborn king.

Then the shepherds left the stable and went into the town to let everyone know about Jesus.

Three wise men from the East had been keeping watch on the stars in the sky. They knew that a great King was to be born. They were waiting for a sign to show where to find Him.

At last, a bright star showed them the way.

They rode across many lands following the star. They thought they would find Him in a palace, but the star led them to a poor stable. They left their camels outside and going in, found Jesus lying in a manger.

At once they knew that He was the one they had been seeking.

Each wise man had brought a present for Jesus which was laid down beside Him.

When they had gone, Mary thought
again for a long time. Why had the
shepherds and the wise men come
so far to see her baby?
Then she picked up
Jesus and held Him
close to her,
thinking about
what the angel
had said.

All these appear in the pages of the story. Can you find them?

Mary   angel   Joseph

donkey   inn-keeper

Jesus

manger

star

shepherds

wise men

Now tell the story in your own words.

The Childhood of Jesus

On a cold, dark night, many years ago, a little baby boy was born. His mother called Him Jesus. The baby's mother was called Mary and her husband was Joseph. Shepherds from nearby and wise men from far lands went to see Jesus because He was a special baby.

The king of the country, which was called Judea, was King Herod. He did not go to see the baby. He was angry when he heard that Jesus was born. It was said that Jesus was to be king over His people. King Herod did not want this king in his country. He had a very cruel plan. All the little children under two years old would be killed. In that way, he could be sure that Jesus would not live.

One night, Joseph had a dream. In
the dream he saw King Herod and
heard his plan. Joseph knew that
the baby Jesus was in great danger.
He heard a kind voice say to him,
"Take Mary and the child away from
this place. Go to Egypt and stay
there until it is safe."

Joseph woke up.
He put all they
needed into a bag
and he untied a
donkey.

Mary woke up too.
She lifted the
baby Jesus and
held Him close to
her.

Then she climbed on to the donkey
and Joseph led them out of the
town.

They walked many miles until they
reached Egypt. There they lived
for a short time.

One day, Joseph heard that King Herod had died. His son had become king in his place. Joseph decided to return to his own land, but to keep away from the big towns. They made their way back to the little town of Nazareth.

There, they unpacked and tried to make their home comfortable. Rugs were laid on the floor.

Mary washed the cooking pots and ground some corn to make bread. Joseph was a carpenter. He began to make wooden tables and yokes for oxen so that he could earn a living.

In this poor, little home, Jesus
grew from a baby to a boy.
When He was about
six years old, He
went to school.

He learned to read and He was told stories about Moses and David. He helped Joseph to put away the tools at the end of the day.

He asked Mary and Joseph many questions. Sometimes, Mary and Joseph were surprised that Jesus knew so much.

Every year, Mary and Joseph went
with the other village people to
the big city of Jerusalem. They
joined together in a special meal.
They sang songs and said prayers
to God.

When the boys were twelve years
old, they could go with their
parents. Jesus was glad when He
could go, too.

It was a long way
to Jerusalem, but
at last they
reached the city
and made camps.

In Jerusalem, there was a large
building called the Temple. Inside
the Temple sat many clever teachers
who read books to the people about
God.

Jesus listened and talked to the teachers for a long time. They were surprised at what He knew.

Jesus decided to stay in the Temple. He slept curled up in a corner near the walls of the Temple and early the next morning, He went inside again.

The other people were packing up
and starting back home.

All day long they walked, stopping
at night to eat and rest.

Mary saw that Jesus
was not with them.
She ran looking
for Jesus, but she
could not find Him.
She was very
worried in case He
had been hurt.

Joseph and Mary
walked all the
way back to
Jerusalem looking
for Jesus.

"Let us go and look in the Temple," said Joseph. "That was the last place where He was seen."

They found Jesus with the teachers, talking and listening.

"We have been so worried about You," said Mary. "Why did You stay behind when we left yesterday?" Jesus said, "I thought you would know that I was in My Father's house and that I have His work to do."

Mary and Joseph were happy they had found Jesus, and they often thought about His words.

All these appear in the pages of
the story. Can you find them?

Jesus

Mary

King Herod

Joseph

dream

Jerusalem

Temple

teachers

Now tell the story in your own words.

Stories Jesus Told

Jesus lived with His family in a village called Nazareth. Mary, His mother, looked after the house. Joseph was a carpenter. He made things out of wood. Jesus helped Joseph each day. When Jesus began teaching, people came from far and near to hear Him speak about God. He told them stories to show them the way God wanted them to live.

One day, Jesus stood on the hillside. The people sat around Him. He spoke to them about a rich man who had two sons. The two boys worked with their father on a farm.

The elder son
helped his father
plant the seeds.
He helped to look
after the pigs
and the sheep.

The younger son
did not like work.
He lay in the
sun and left the
others to do all
the hard work.

One day, the younger son said to his father, "I do not want to stay here. I want to be with my friends. Give me my share of the farm. I do not want to wait until I am old."

His father was very sad. He did not want to see his son go away. At last he gave him some money.

He waved to his son as he went away across the fields. He did not know if he would ever see him again.

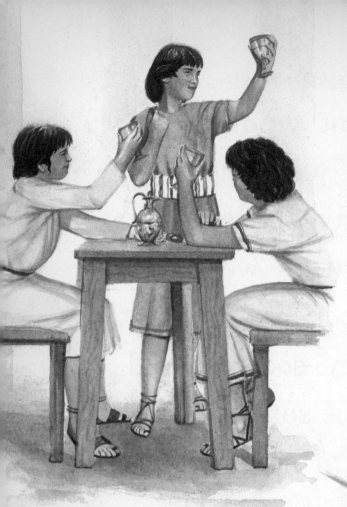

At first, the boy was very happy. He bought himself fine clothes. He went out with his friends, eating and drinking.

Soon, he had spent all his money. His friends went away and left him. He was very lonely.

He went to many places looking for work. He was very hungry. A farmer gave him the job of looking after his pigs.

He was so hungry that he even wanted the food that was given to the pigs.

One day, as he sat on the hot
dusty ground, watching the pigs, he
said, "I will go home to my father.
I am very sorry for what I have
done. My father looks after his
servants better than this. Maybe
he will let me be his servant."

Now his father
was a very kind
man. Every day
he went to the
top of the hill
to see if his
son was coming
home.
One day, very
far away he
saw someone
coming. He
was sure it
was his son.

He ran to the servants, saying "Make a feast for everyone. At last my son has come home. Bring out my best cloak for him to wear."

The elder son had been hard at work. He heard his father's words. He was very upset. It did not seem fair. He had stayed at home to help on the farm. He had worked very hard. His brother had wasted his time and his money. Now his father was pleased to see his brother. He was making a feast for his lazy son!

The father saw that his son was angry. He put his arms around him. He said to him, "Come, let us all be happy together. I thought your brother had gone for good. He was lost and now he is found."

Jesus wanted to teach the people that God loves everyone – no matter what she or he may have done.

Another story Jesus told is called
The Good Samaritan.

One day, a trader was on his way
from one town to another. It was
a long, hard journey. Many people
had been attacked by robbers. The
robbers hid in the caves dug out
of the rocky hillside.

As the man went on his way, robbers came from behind some rocks. They hit him with their sticks.

The man fell to the ground. He was hurt and bleeding. They took all his money and his donkey. They ran away.

Soon a priest came by, on his way to the Temple. "Is that man dead?" he asked. "If I stop, I shall not be able to go to the Temple."

So he did not stop. He went by on the other side of the road.

After a while, another man came by, on his donkey. He was going to sing in the Temple. He saw the poor man lying there in the hot sun. He too passed by. He looked the other way.

A little later, a man from the land called Samaria came by.

He stopped when he saw the man
lying on the ground. He saw that
the man was badly hurt.
The Samaritan washed the man's cuts
and put a clean cloth over them.
He helped the man on to his donkey.

Slowly they went on their way until
they came to an inn.

The Samaritan spoke to the inn-keeper. He said, "Please look after this man. He has been beaten. All his goods have been stolen. Here is some money to pay you. I will come this way again. If you need more money, I will give it to you then."

The Samaritan went on his way.

Jesus said to the people, "Which man would you have to be your friend?" They said, "The Samaritan because he helped the man who was hurt." "Yes," said Jesus. "Now you must go and always help those who cannot help themselves."

Jesus told many more stories. The stories Jesus told are called parables.

All these appear in the pages of the story. Can you find them?

hillside

sons

feast

father

trader

robbers

Samaritan

priest

Now tell the story in your own words.

Standing on the Promises

R. K. C.

R. Kelso Carter

1. Stand-ing on the prom-is-es of Christ my King, Thro' e-ter-nal
2. Stand-ing on the prom-is-es that can-not fail, When the howl-ing
3. Stand-ing on the prom-is-es I now can see Per-fect, pres-ent
4. Stand-ing on the prom-is-es of Christ the Lord, Bound to Him e-
5. Stand-ing on the prom-is-es I can-not fall, Lis-t'ning ev-'ry

a-ges let His prais-es ring; Glo-ry in the highest I will shout and sing,
storms of doubt and fear as-sail, By the liv-ing Word of God I shall pre-vail,
cleansing in the blood for me; Standing in the lib-erty where Christ makes free,
ter-nal-ly by love's strong cord, O-ver-com-ing dai-ly with the Spir-it's sword,
mo-ment to the Spir-it's call, Rest-ing in my Sav-ior, as my all in all,

Chorus

Standing on the promis-es of God. Stand-ing, stand-ing,
Standing on the promises, Standing on the promises.

Stand-ing on the promis-es of God my Sav-ior; Stand-ing,
Standing on the prom-is-es.

stand-ing, I'm stand-ing on the prom-is-es of God.
Stand-ing on the prom-is-es,

Bringing in the Sheaves

George A. Minor

1. Sow-ing in the morn-ing, sow-ing seeds of kind-ness, Sow-ing in the
2. Sow-ing in the sun-shine, sow-ing in the shad-ows, Fear-ing nei-ther
3. Go-ing forth with weep-ing, sow-ing for the Mas-ter, Tho' the loss sus-

noon-tide and the dew-y eve; Wait-ing for the har-vest,
clouds nor win-ter's chill-ing breeze; By and by the har-vest,
tained our spir-it oft-en grieves; When our weep-ing's o-ver,

and the time of reap-ing, We shall come re-joic-ing, bring-ing in the sheaves.
and the la-bor end-ed, We shall come re-joic-ing, bring-ing in the sheaves.
He will bid us wel-come, We shall come re-joic-ing, bring-ing in the sheaves.

CHORUS

Bring-ing in the sheaves, bring-ing in the sheaves, We shall come re-joic-
Bring-ing in the sheaves, bring-ing in the sheaves, We shall come re-joic-

1
ing, bring-ing in the sheaves;
2
ing, bring-ing in the sheaves.

A Charge to Keep I Have

Charles Wesley

Lowell Mason

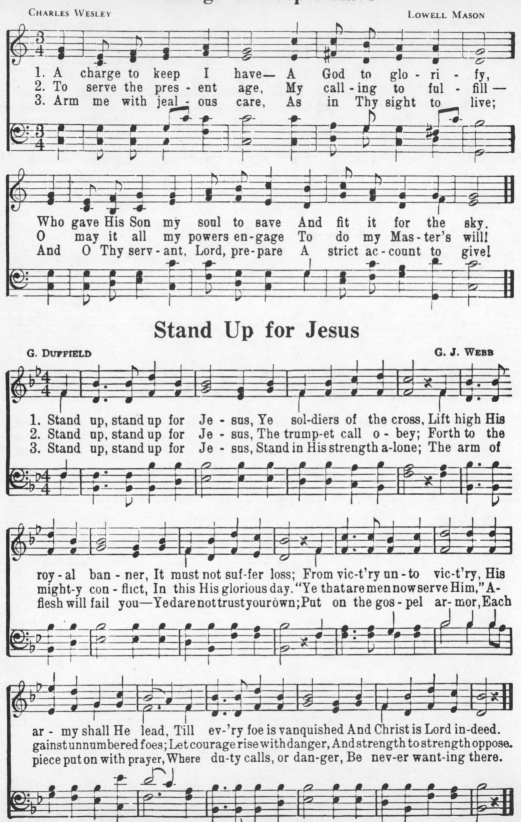

1. A charge to keep I have— A God to glo-ri-fy,
2. To serve the pres-ent age, My call-ing to ful-fill—
3. Arm me with jeal-ous care, As in Thy sight to live;

Who gave His Son my soul to save And fit it for the sky.
O may it all my powers en-gage To do my Mas-ter's will!
And O Thy serv-ant, Lord, pre-pare A strict ac-count to give!

Stand Up for Jesus

G. Duffield

G. J. Webb

1. Stand up, stand up for Je-sus, Ye sol-diers of the cross, Lift high His
2. Stand up, stand up for Je-sus, The trump-et call o-bey; Forth to the
3. Stand up, stand up for Je-sus, Stand in His strength a-lone; The arm of

roy-al ban-ner, It must not suf-fer loss; From vic-t'ry un-to vic-t'ry, His
might-y con-flict, In this His glorious day. "Ye that are men now serve Him," A-
flesh will fail you—Ye dare not trust your own; Put on the gos-pel ar-mor, Each

ar-my shall He lead, Till ev-'ry foe is vanquished And Christ is Lord in-deed.
gainst unnumbered foes; Let courage rise with danger, And strength to strength oppose.
piece put on with prayer, Where du-ty calls, or dan-ger, Be nev-er want-ing there.

America the Beautiful

KATHERINE LEE BATES

SAMUEL A. WARD

1. O beau - ti - ful for spa-cious skies, For am - ber waves of grain,
2. O beau - ti - ful for pil - grim feet, Whose stern, im-pas-sioned stress
3. O beau - ti - ful for he-roes proved In lib - er - at - ing strife,
4. O beau - ti - ful for pa-triot dream That sees be - yond the years

For pur - ple moun-tain maj - es - ties A - bove the fruit - ed plain!
A thor-ough-fare for free - dom beat A - cross the wil - der - ness!
Who more than self their coun-try loved, And mer - cy more than life!
Thine al - a - bas - ter cit - ies gleam, Undimmed by hu - man tears!

A - mer - i - ca! A - mer - i - ca! God shed His grace on thee,
A - mer - i - ca! A - mer - i - ca! God mend thine ev - 'ry flaw,
A - mer - i - ca! A - mer - i - ca! May God thy gold re - fine,
A - mer - i - ca! A - mer - i - ca! God shed His grace on thee,

And crown thy good with broth - er-hood From sea to shin - ing sea!
Con - firm thy soul in self - con-trol, Thy lib - er - ty in law!
Till all suc - cess be no - ble-ness And ev - 'ry gain di - vine!
And crown thy good with broth - er-hood From sea to shin - ing sea!

The Star-Spangled Banner

Francis Scott Key

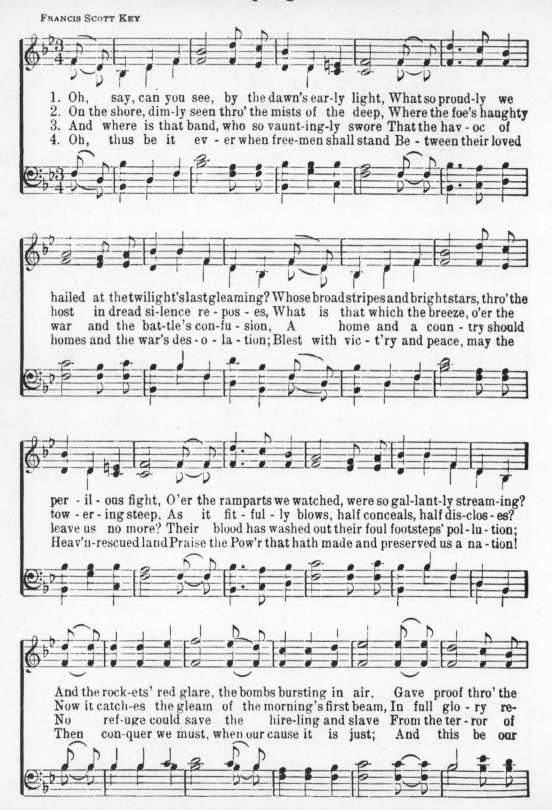

1. Oh, say, can you see, by the dawn's ear-ly light, What so proud-ly we
2. On the shore, dim-ly seen thro' the mists of the deep, Where the foe's haughty
3. And where is that band, who so vaunt-ing-ly swore That the hav-oc of
4. Oh, thus be it ev-er when free-men shall stand Be-tween their loved

hailed at the twilight's last gleaming? Whose broad stripes and bright stars, thro' the
host in dread si-lence re-pos-es, What is that which the breeze, o'er the
war and the bat-tle's con-fu-sion, A home and a coun-try should
homes and the war's des-o-la-tion; Blest with vic-t'ry and peace, may the

per-il-ous fight, O'er the ramparts we watched, were so gal-lant-ly stream-ing?
tow-er-ing steep, As it fit-ful-ly blows, half conceals, half dis-clos-es?
leave us no more? Their blood has washed out their foul footsteps' pol-lu-tion;
Heav'n-rescued land Praise the Pow'r that hath made and preserved us a na-tion!

And the rock-ets' red glare, the bombs bursting in air, Gave proof thro' the
Now it catch-es the gleam of the morning's first beam, In full glo-ry re-
No ref-uge could save the hire-ling and slave From the ter-ror of
Then con-quer we must, when our cause it is just; And this be our

The Star-Spangled Banner

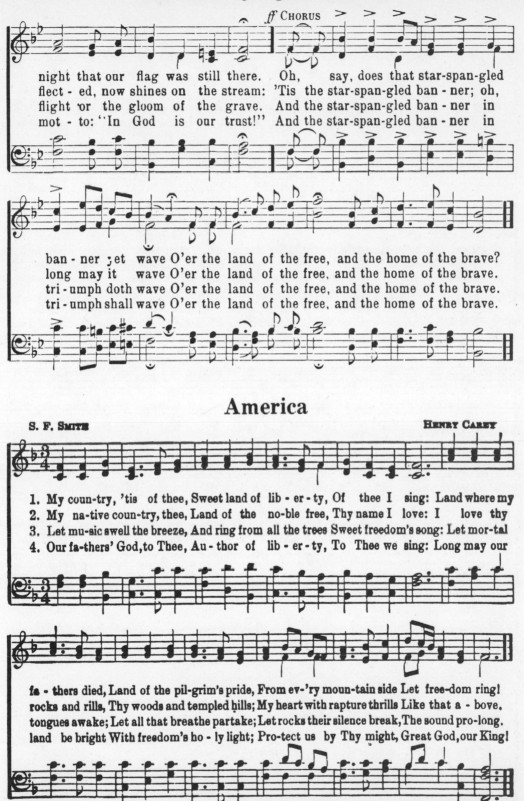

ff CHORUS

night that our flag was still there. Oh, say, does that star-span-gled
flect - ed, now shines on the stream: 'Tis the star-span-gled ban - ner; oh,
flight 'or the gloom of the grave. And the star-span-gled ban - ner in
mot - to: "In God is our trust!" And the star-span-gled ban - ner in

ban - ner ;et wave O'er the land of the free, and the home of the brave?
long may it wave O'er the land of the free, and the home of the brave.
tri - umph doth wave O'er the land of the free, and the home of the brave.
tri - umph shall wave O'er the land of the free, and the home of the brave.

America

S. F. SMITH   HENRY CAREY

1. My coun-try, 'tis of thee, Sweet land of lib-er-ty, Of thee I sing: Land where my
2. My na-tive coun-try, thee, Land of the no-ble free, Thy name I love: I love thy
3. Let mu-sic swell the breeze, And ring from all the trees Sweet freedom's song: Let mor-tal
4. Our fa-thers' God, to Thee, Au-thor of lib-er-ty, To Thee we sing: Long may our

fa - thers died, Land of the pil-grim's pride, From ev-'ry moun-tain side Let free-dom ring!
rocks and rills, Thy woods and templed hills; My heart with rapture thrills Like that a - bove.
tongues awake; Let all that breathe partake; Let rocks their silence break, The sound pro-long.
land be bright With freedom's ho - ly light; Pro-tect us by Thy might, Great God, our King!

Jesus Loves the Little Children

Rev. C. H. Woolston, D. D.

Geo. F. Root

1. Je - sus calls the chil-dren dear, "Come to Me and nev - er fear, For I
2. Je - sus is the Shep-herd true, And He'll al-ways stand by you, For He
3. I am com-ing, Lord, to Thee, And Thy sol-dier I will be, For He

love the lit - tle chil-dren of the world; I will take you by the hand,
loves the lit - tle chil-dren of the world; He's a Sav - ior great and strong,
loves the lit - tle chil-dren of the world; And His cross I'll al-ways bear,

Lead you to the bet - ter land, For I love the lit - tle
And He'll shield you from the wrong, For He loves the lit - tle
And for Him I'll do and dare, For He loves the lit - tle

CHORUS

chil-dren of the world."
chil-dren of the world.   Je - sus loves the lit - tle chil - dren,
chil-dren of the world.   lit - tle chil - dren,

All the chil-dren of the world;   Red and yel-low, black and white, They are
All the chil - dren of the world;

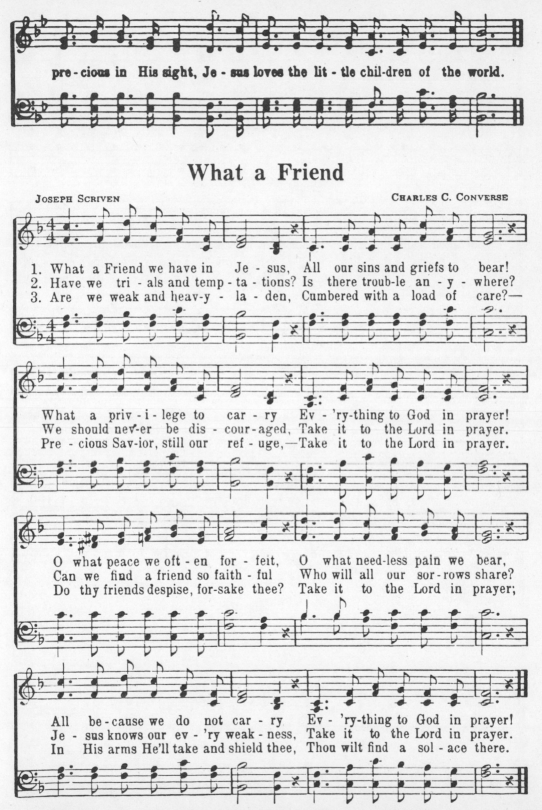

pre - cious in His sight, Je - sus loves the lit - tle chil-dren of the world.

What a Friend

JOSEPH SCRIVEN

CHARLES C. CONVERSE

1. What a Friend we have in Je - sus, All our sins and griefs to bear!
2. Have we tri - als and temp - ta - tions? Is there troub-le an - y - where?
3. Are we weak and heav-y - la - den, Cumbered with a load of care?—

What a priv-i-lege to car - ry Ev - 'ry-thing to God in prayer!
We should nev-er be dis - cour-aged, Take it to the Lord in prayer.
Pre - cious Sav-ior, still our ref - uge,—Take it to the Lord in prayer.

O what peace we oft - en for - feit, O what need-less pain we bear,
Can we find a friend so faith - ful Who will all our sor-rows share?
Do thy friends despise, for-sake thee? Take it to the Lord in prayer;

All be-cause we do not car - ry Ev - 'ry-thing to God in prayer!
Je - sus knows our ev - 'ry weak - ness, Take it to the Lord in prayer.
In His arms He'll take and shield thee, Thou wilt find a sol - ace there.

Count Your Blessings

Rev. Johnson Oatman, Jr.

E. O. Excell

1. When up-on life's bil-lows you are tem-pest-tossed, When you are dis-
2. Are you ev-er bur-dened with a load of care? Does the cross seem
3. When you look at oth-ers with their lands and gold, Think that Christ has
4. So, a-mid the con-flict, whether great or small, Do not be dis-

cour-aged, think-ing all is lost, Count your man-y bless-ings, name them
heav-y you are called to bear? Count your man-y bless-ings, ev-'ry
prom-ised you His wealth un-told; Count your man-y bless-ings, mon-ey
cour-aged, God is o-ver all; Count your man-y bless-ings, an-gels

one by one, And it will sur-prise you what the Lord hath done.
doubt will fly, And you will be sing-ing as the days go by.
can-not buy Your re-ward in heav-en, nor your home on high.
will at-tend, Help and com-fort give you to your jour-ney's end.

Chorus.

Count your bless-ings, Name them one by one; Count your
Count your man-y bless-ings, Name them one by one; Count your man-y

bless-ings, See what God hath done; Count your bless-ings,
bless-ings, See what God hath done; Count your man-y bless-ings,

Count Your Blessings

Name them one by one; Count your man-y blessings, See what God hath done.

Jesus Loves Me

Anna B. Warner, alt.

Wm. B. Bradbury.

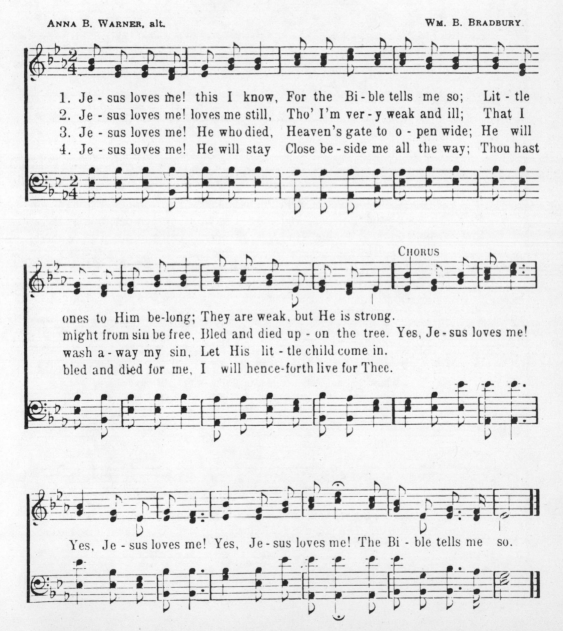

1. Je - sus loves me! this I know, For the Bi - ble tells me so; Lit - tle
2. Je - sus loves me! loves me still, Tho' I'm ver - y weak and ill; That I
3. Je - sus loves me! He who died, Heaven's gate to o - pen wide; He will
4. Je - sus loves me! He will stay Close be - side me all the way; Thou hast

ones to Him be-long; They are weak, but He is strong.
might from sin be free, Bled and died up - on the tree. Yes, Je - sus loves me!
wash a - way my sin, Let His lit - tle child come in.
bled and died for me, I will hence-forth live for Thee.

CHORUS

Yes, Je - sus loves me! Yes, Je - sus loves me! The Bi - ble tells me so.

When the Roll is Called Up Yonder

J. M. B.   J. M. BLACK

1. When the trumpet of the Lord shall sound, and time shall be no more, And the
2. On that bright and cloudless morning when the dead in Christ shall rise, And the
3. Let us la - bor for the Mas - ter from the dawn till set-ting sun, Let us

morning breaks, e-ter-nal, bright and fair; When the saved of earth shall gather
glo - ry of His res - ur-rec-tion share; When His cho-sen ones shall gather
talk of all His wondrous love and care; Then when all of life is o - ver,

o - ver on the oth-er shore, And the roll is called up yon-der, I'll be there.
to their home beyond the skies, And the roll is called up yon-der, I'll be there.
and our work on earth is done, And the roll is called up yon-der, I'll be there.

CHORUS.

When the roll . . . . . . is called up yon - - - - der, When the
When the roll is called up yon - der, I'll be there,

roll . . . . is called up yon - - der, When the roll . . . . is called up
When the roll is called up yon-der, I'll be there,   When the roll is called up

When the Roll is Called Up Yonder

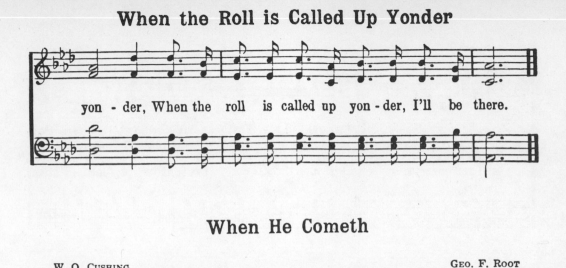

yon - der, When the roll is called up yon - der, I'll be there.

When He Cometh

W. O. CUSHING

GEO. F. ROOT

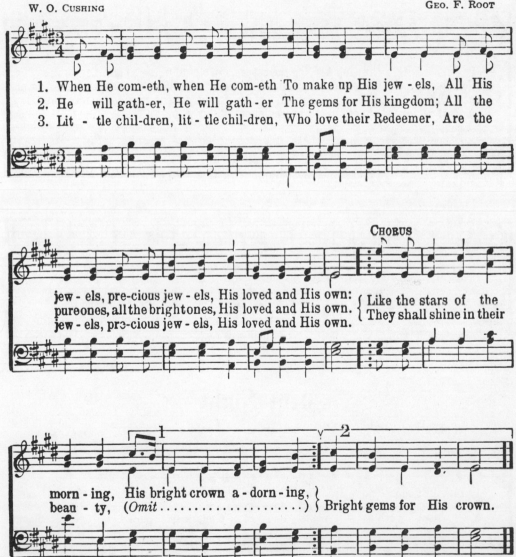

1. When He com-eth, when He com-eth To make up His jew-els, All His
2. He will gath-er, He will gath-er The gems for His kingdom; All the
3. Lit - tle chil-dren, lit - tle chil-dren, Who love their Redeemer, Are the

CHORUS

jew - els, pre-cious jew - els, His loved and His own: } Like the stars of the
pure ones, all the bright ones, His loved and His own. } They shall shine in their
jew - els, pre-cious jew - els, His loved and His own.

morn - ing, His bright crown a-dorn - ing, } Bright gems for His crown.
beau - ty, (Omit . . . .)

The First Noel

Traditional
Traditional

1. The first No - el   the angel did say Was to certain poor shepherds in fields as they lay;
2. And by   the light of that same Star, Three wise men came from country far;
3. This Star drew nigh to the northwest, O'er Beth - le-hem   it took its rest,
4. Then enter-ed in those wise men three, Full rev-'rent-ly   up-on their knee,

In fields where they lay keeping their sheep, On a cold winter's night that was so deep.
To seek for a King was their in - tent, And to follow the Star wherever it went.
And there it   did both stop and stay, Right o-ver the place where Jesus lay.
And of - fered there in His pres-ence, Their gold, and myrrh, and frank-incense.

REFRAIN.

No - el, No - el, No - el, No - el, Born is the King of Is - ra - el.

Silent Night

Joseph Mohr
P. M.
Franz Gruber

1. Si - lent night! ho - ly night! All   is   calm, all   is   bright 'Round yon
2. Si - lent night! ho - ly night! Shep-herds quake at   the sight! Glo - ries
3. Si - lent night! ho - ly night! Son of   God, love's pure light Ra - diant

Silent Night

vir - gin moth - er and Child! Ho - ly In-fant, so ten-der and mild,
stream from heaven a - far, Heav'n-ly hosts sing Al - le - lu - ia;
beams from Thy ho - ly face, With the dawn of re - deem - ing grace,

Sleep in heav - en - ly peace, Sleep in heav - en - ly peace.
Christ, the Sav - ior, is born, Christ, the Sav - ior, is born.
Je - sus, Lord, at Thy birth, Je - sus, Lord, at Thy birth. A - men.

Away in a Manger

Martin Luther   Martin Luther

1. A - way in a man - ger, No crib for a bed, The lit - tle Lord
2. The cat - tle are low - ing, The Ba - by a - wakes, But lit - tle Lord
3. Be near me, Lord Je - sus, I ask Thee to stay Close by me for-

Je - sus Laid down His sweet head; The stars in the sky Looked
Je - sus, No cry - ing He makes; I love Thee, Lord Je - sus! Look
ev - er, And love me, I pray; Bless all the dear chil-dren In

down where He lay,—The lit - tle Lord Je - sus, A - sleep on the hay.
down from the sky, And stay by my cra - dle, Till morn-ing is nigh.
Thy ten - der care, Pre - pare us for heav - en, To live with Thee there.

O Little Town of Bethlehem

PHILLIPS BROOKS

LEWIS H. REDNER

1. O lit-tle town of Beth-le-hem, How still we see thee lie;
2. For Christ is born of Ma - ry; And gath-ered all a - bove,
3. How si-lent-ly, how si-lent-ly, The won-drous gift is giv'n!
4. O ho-ly Child of Beth-le-hem, De-scend on us, we pray;

A - bove thy deep and dreamless sleep The si - lent stars go by:
While mor-tals sleep, the an-gels keep Their watch of wond'ring love.
So God im-parts to hu-man hearts The bless-ings of His heav'n.
Cast out our sin, and en-ter in, Be born in us to - day.

Yet in thy dark streets shin-eth The ev-er-last-ing Light; The
O morn-ing stars, to-geth-er Pro-claim the ho-ly birth; And
No ear may hear His com-ing, But in this world of sin, Where
We hear the Christ-mas an-gels The great glad ti-dings tell; O

hopes and fears of all the years Are met in thee to-night.
prais-es sing to God the King, And peace to men on earth.
meek souls will re-ceive Him still, The dear Christ en-ters in.
come to us, a - bide with us, Our Lord Em-man-u-el. A-men.

Joy to the World!

Isaac Watts

Arr. from George F. Handel

1. Joy to the world! the Lord is come; Let earth re-
2. Joy to the world! the Sav - ior reigns; Let men their
3. No more let sins and sor - rows grow, Nor thorns in-
4. He rules the world with truth and grace, And makes the

ceive her King; Let ev - 'ry heart pre - pare Him room,
songs em - ploy; While fields and floods, rocks, hills and plains
fest the ground; He comes to make His bless - ings flow
na - tions prove The glo - ries of His right-eous - ness,

And heav'n and na - ture sing, And heav'n and na - ture
Re - peat the sound - ing joy, Re - peat the sound - ing
Far as the curse is found, Far as the curse is
And won - ders of His love, And won - ders of His

1. And heav'n and na - ture sing,.......... And

sing, And heav'n, and heav'n and na - ture sing.
joy, Re - peat, re - peat the sound - ing joy.
found, Far as, far as the curse is found.
love, And won - ders, and won - ders of His love.
heav'n and na - ture sing,